MW00716477

*To Mother with Love*

# To Mother with Love

Edited by Kevin Osborn

Ariel Books

Andrews and McMeel
Kansas City

Book design by Maura Fadden Rosenthal

ISBN: 0-8362-4720-5

Library of Congress Catalog Card Number: 94-71134

10 9 8 7 6 5 4 3 2

Illustrations: Frontispiece: Dorthea and Francesca, Cecelia Beaux, 1898; pp: 6, 14,
22, 28, 36: Still Life: Flowers and Fruit, (details) Severin Roesen, circa 1850-
1855; p. 8: A Frolic, Isaac Snowman, circa 1905; p. 11: Le berceau (The Cradle),
Berthe Morisot, 1972; p. 12: Lady Cockburn and Her Children, Sir Joshua
Reynolds, 1773; p. 16: The Elder Sister, William A. Bouguereau, 1864; p. 20:
Mère et enfant (Mother and Baby, vi-8), Mary Cassatt, 1880; p. 31: Madame
Vigée-Lebrun and Child (in Greek Toga), Elisabeth Vigée-Lebrun, 1789; p. 40:
Feeding the Pigeons, George Sheridan Knowles, circa 1915.

# Contents

# Tales of Motherhood

I am all the time talking about you, and bragging, to one person or another. I am like the Ancient Mariner, who had a tale in his heart he must unfold to all. I am always buttonholing somebody and saying, "Someday you must meet my mother."

—Edna St. Vincent Millay

John Wesley, the founder of Methodism, recalled his father once asking his mother, "How can you have the patience to tell that blockhead John the same thing twenty times over?"

"Why, Samuel," Susanna Wesley wisely explained, "if I had told him only nineteen times, I would have wasted my breath."

Two women, each claiming a newborn baby was hers, were brought before Solomon, king of Israel. Solomon ordered the baby to be cut in two and each woman be given half. One woman accepted this decision but the second begged the king to give the other woman the living child and "in no wise slay it." Recognizing in this plea the real mother's love for her child, Solomon commanded that the baby be given to her.

In ancient Rome, a guest eagerly showed off her priceless jewelry to her host, Cornelia. "And where are your jewels, my dear?" the ostentatious guest asked. "Might I see them?"

Cornelia immediately called in her two sons, Tiberius and Gaius Gracchus, who would later grow up to reform Rome's agrarian laws. "These are my jewels," the proud mother said, "in which I alone delight."

While conquering Persia and expanding the Macedonian Empire, Alexander the Great boasted of his divine right to rule the world, often claiming he was a god since his father was Jupiter, the chief god of the Romans. Alexander's mother, Olympias, diplomatically refused to confirm or deny her son's grandiose claim, saying she didn't want "to get into any trouble with Juno," Jupiter's wife.

Edgar Paine, a friend of the English writer Samuel Butler, loved to tell people about his daughter's excited reaction when he told her she had a new baby sister. "Does Mama know?" the six-year-old wondered. "Let's go and tell her."

Cary Grant's mother telephoned her son to praise one of his television performances—as well as chastise him for not dyeing his hair. The urbane actor affably insisted he didn't mind his hair going gray. "But it bothers me," his mother, then in her nineties, snapped. "It makes me seem so old."

During the Revolutionary War, General George Washington once ordered his soldiers to commandeer as many horses as they could find in the surrounding Virginia farms and villages. However, when one soldier informed the owner of a nearby plantation he had come to confiscate her horses, the elderly woman refused, explaining that she needed them to plow her fields.

"Under whose orders do you claim my horses?" she asked.

"General George Washington," the soldier proudly replied.

"Well," the woman smiled, "you tell General George Washington that his mother says he cannot have her horses."

# On Motherhood

Though motherhood is the most important of all the professions—requiring more knowledge than any other department in human affairs—there was no attention given to preparation for this office.

—Elizabeth Cady Stanton

*S*ometimes the strength of motherhood is greater than natural laws.

—Barbara Kingsolver

*A*nd so our mothers and grandmothers have, more often than not, anonymously handed on the creative spark, the seed of the flower they themselves never hoped to see— or like a sealed letter they could not plainly read.

—Alice Walker

*Probably* there is nothing in human nature more resonant with charges than the flow of energy between two biologically alike bodies, one of which has lain in amniotic bliss inside the other, one of which has labored to give birth to the other. The materials are here for the deepest mutuality and the most painful estrangement.

—Adrienne Rich

*Adorable* children are considered to be the general property of the human race. (Rude children belong to their mothers.)

—Judith Martin

And wherever we may turn,
This lesson we shall learn,
A boy's best friend is his mother.

—Joseph P. Skelley

The God to whom little boys say their prayers has a face very much like their mother's.

—Sir James M. Barrie

What do girls do who haven't any mothers to help them through their troubles?

—Louisa May Alcott

Youth fades; love droops; the leaves of friendship fall:
A mother's secret love outlives them all.

—Oliver Wendell Holmes

She never outgrows the burden of love, and to the end she carries the weight of hope for those she bore.

—Florida Scott-Maxwell

A mother is a person who seeing there are only four pieces of pie for five people, promptly announces she never did care for pie.

—Tenneva Jordan

What are Raphael's Madonnas but the shadow of a mother's love, fixed in permanent outline forever?

—Thomas Wentworth Higginson

Every mother is like Moses. She does not enter the promised land. She prepares a world she will not see.

—Pope Paul VI

*A* suburban mother's role is to deliver children obstetrically once, and by car for ever after.

—Peter de Vries

*I* think it must somewhere be written, that the virtues of mothers shall be visited on their children.

—Charles Dickens

The mother's battle for her child—with sickness, with poverty, with war, with all the forces of exploitation and callousness that cheapen human life—needs to become a common human battle, waged in love and in the passion for survival.

—Adrienne Rich


Raising children is far more creative than most jobs around for men and women.

—Benjamin Spock


Perhaps the greatest social service that can be rendered by anybody to the country and to mankind is to bring up a family. But here again, because there is nothing to sell, there is a very general disposition to regard a married woman's work as no work at all, and to take it as a matter of course that she should not be paid for it.

—George Bernard Shaw

# On Being a Mother

For me, motherhood has been the one true, great, and wholly successful romance. It is the only love I have known that is expansive and that could have stretched to contain with equal passion more than one object.

—Irma Kurtz

*H*ousewives and mothers seldom find it practicable to come out on strike. They have no union, anyway.

—Elaine Morgan

*T*he most effective form of birth control I know is spending the day with my kids.

—Jill Bensley

*L*ike so many things one did for children, it was absurd but pleasing, and the pleasure came from the anticipation of their pleasure.

—Mary Gordon

*L*oving a child doesn't mean giving in to all his whims; to love him is to bring out the best in him, to teach him to love what is difficult.

—Nadia Boulanger

*O*ver the years I have learned that motherhood is much like an austere religious order, the joining of which obligates one to relinquish all claims to personal possessions.

—Nancy Stahl

*I* long to put the experience of fifty years at once into your young lives, to give you at once the key of that treasure chamber every gem of which has cost me tears and struggles and prayers, but you must work for these inward treasures yourselves.

—Harriet Beecher Stowe

*O*n one thing professionals and amateurs agree: mothers can't win.

—Margaret Drabble

*I* figure if the kids are alive at the end of the day, I've done my job.

—Roseanne Arnold

*T*he phrase "working mother" is redundant.

—Jane Sellman

*W*omen do not have to sacrifice personhood if they are mothers. They do not have to sacrifice motherhood in order to be persons.

—Elaine Heffer

*M*ore than in any other human relationship, overwhelmingly more, motherhood means being instantly interruptible, responsive, responsible . . .

—Tillie Olsen

"You almost died," a nurse told her. But that was nonsense. Of course she wouldn't have died; she had children. When you have children, you're obligated to live.

—Anne Tyler

She had found that the more the child demanded of her, the more she had to give. Strength came up in waves that had their source in a sea of calm and unconquerable devotion. The child's holy trust made her open her eyes, and she took stock of herself and found that everything was all right, and that she could meet what challenges arose and meet them well, and that she had nothing to apologize for—on the contrary, she had every reason to rejoice.

—Maeve Brennan

# On My Mother

My mother is a poem I'll never be able to write
though everything I write is a poem to my mother.
—Sharon Doubiago

*Mama! Dearest mama! I know you are my one true friend.*

—Nikolai Gogol

*I had a Mother who read me things
That wholesome life to the boy heart brings—
Stories that stir with an upward touch,
Oh, that each mother of boys were such!*

*You may have tangible wealth untold;
Caskets of jewels and coffers of gold.
Richer than I you can never be—
I had a Mother who read to me.*

—Strickland Gillilan

*Mama exhorted her children at every opportunity to "jump at de sun." We might not land on the sun, but at least we would get off the ground.*

—Zora Neale Hurston

Mother, dear mother, the years have been long
Since I last listened your lullaby song:
Sing, then, and unto my soul it shall seem
Womanhood's years have been only a dream.
Clasped to your heart in a loving embrace,
With your light lashes just sweeping my face,
Never hereafter to wake or to weep;—
Rock me to sleep, mother,—rock me to sleep!

—Elizabeth Akers Allen

$\mathcal{I}$ know how the mind rushes back . . . to infancy, when those stiffened hands were wrapped around us in twining love; when that bosom was the pillow of our first sorrows; when those ears . . . heard our whispered confidence; when those eyes . . . watched our every motion.

—Caroline Gilman

$\mathcal{M}$y mother had a great deal of trouble with me, but I think she enjoyed it.

—Mark Twain

$\mathcal{M}$y mother loved children—she would have given anything if I had been one.

—Groucho Marx

She always leaned to watch for us,
Anxious if we were late,
In winter by the window,
In summer by the gate;

And though we mocked her tenderly,
Who had such foolish care,
The long way home would seem more safe
Because she waited there.

—Margaret Widdemer

I cannot forget my mother. Though not as sturdy as others, she is my bridge. When I needed to get across, she steadied herself long enough for me to run across safely.

—Renita Weems

Let me not forget that I am the daughter of a woman who bent her head, trembling, between the blades of a cactus, her wrinkled face full of ecstasy over the promise of a flower, a woman who herself never ceased to flower, untiringly, during three quarters of a century.

—Colette

When mamma smiled, beautiful as her face was, it grew incomparably more lovely, and everything around seemed brighter. If in life's sad moments I could but have had a glimpse of that smile I should not have known what sorrow is.

—Leo Tolstoy

When I stopped seeing my mother with the eyes of a child, I saw the woman who helped me give birth to myself.

—Nancy Friday

$\mathscr{N}$ow that I am in my forties, she tells me I'm beautiful . . . and we have the long, personal and even remarkably honest phone calls I always wanted so intensely I forbade myself to imagine them. . . . With my poems, I finally won even my mother. The longest wooing of my life.

—Marge Piercy

$\mathscr{I}$'m never going to write my autobiography and it's all my mother's fault. I didn't hate her, so I have practically no material. In fact, the situation is worse than I'm pretending. We were crazy about her—and you know I'll never get a book out of that, much less a musical.

—Jean Kerr

# Other Mothers

According to some creation myths, "Mother Night," who represents the darkness of the womb, in which all things are created, and infinite space, the source of all heavenly bodies, laid the silver egg of the cosmos and gave birth to all the gods.

*R*osa Parks, the "Mother of the Civil Rights Movement," is the black seamstress whose arrest for refusing to give up her seat to a white person on a segregated bus became the catalyst for the 1955 bus strike in Montgomery, Alabama. This strike laid the groundwork for the Supreme Court's ruling unconstitutional all laws permitting segregation.

*M*ary Harris Jones, "Labor's Joan of Arc," was given the name "Mother Jones" for speaking out against the horrors of child labor during the late 1800s and for organizing miners' wives to stand guard at mine entrances armed with brooms and babies to fend off strikebreakers.

The phrase "Mother Earth," according to Roman legend, was first used by Junius Brutus, ancestor of the Brutus who was one of Caesar's assassins. Upon hearing from the Oracle at Delphi that "he who should first kiss his mother" would become the next ruler, Brutus immediately flung himself to the ground with "I kiss thee, Mother Earth!" Evidently the Oracle got his gist, for Brutus went on to become the founder of the Roman Republic.

Old Mother Hubbard was the housekeeper for a member of Parliament during the reign of George III. She and her bare cupboard were made famous in a thirteen-stanza poem by Sarah Martin, who almost married one of George's sons, William IV.

As the ascribed authoress of English nursery rhymes, "Mother Goose" may be undisputed, but the origin of her name is not. Some say it came from Charlemagne's mother, Queen Goosefoot, a patron of children. Others claim it came from Elizabeth Vergoose, the American mother-in-law of Thomas Fleet, who published Mother Goose's Melodies in her honor.